THE HORROR OF WORLD WAR I

by Nancy Dickmann

Consultant: Philip Parker
Author and historian

capstone

Infosearch books are published by Capstone Press,
1710 Roe Crest Drive, North Mankato, Minnesota 56003
www.mycapstone.com

Library of Congress Cataloging-in-Publication Data
Library of Congress Cataloging-in-Publication data is available on the Library of Congress website.

978-1-4846-4168-2 (library binding)
978-1-4846-4172-9 (paperback)
978-1-4846-4176-7 (eBook PDF)

Editorial Credits
Editor: Nancy Dickmann
Designer: Rocket Design (East Anglia) Ltd
Production Specialist: Kathy McColley
Media Researchers: Nancy Dickmann,
Steve White-Thomson, and Izzi Howell
Illustrators: Rocket Design (East Anglia) Ltd and Ron Dixon

Photo Credits
Alamy: akg-images, 35, 40, Chris Hellier, 16, Chronicle, 42, Everett Collection Historical, 37, IanDagnall Computing, 7, John Frost Newspapers, 31, PF-(wararchive), 41, Simon Dack, 21, Trinity Mirror/Mirrorpix, 15, World History Archive, 1, 23, iStock Photo: ijeweb, 43, richjem, 14, Shutterstock: Aksenenko Olga, 3 (dirt), 44 (dirt), Andre Nantel, 19, Everett Historical, 4, 6, 9, 10, 11, 12, 13, 18, 20, 22, 24, 25, 26, 27 (aeroplanes), 27 (Red Baron), 32, 33, 34, 36, 38, 39, LighteniR, 23 (explosion), Martial Red, 4 (skull and crossbones), Seita, 10 (silhouetted soldiers), 20 (silhouetted soldiers), Vladvm, 25 (ship outline), Willequet Manuel, 5, YamabikaY, 3 (bullet), Zsolt Horvath, 17, Superstock: Science and Society, 29, World History Archive, cover.

Printed in the United States of America.
010365F17

Table of Contents

What Was World War I?

From 1914 to 1918, a brutal war raged across the world. Its battles were fought on three continents. Soldiers from dozens of countries fought on land, at sea, and even in the air, using recently invented airplanes.

More than 65 million soldiers were involved. Most were European, but troops came from as far away as New Zealand. Millions of **civilians** were also drawn into the conflict. At the time, the conflict was simply called "The Great War" or the "World War." People didn't start calling it "World War I" until 1939, when the next world war began.

■ Fighting in World War I was deadly. The landscape was churned into a sea of mud and blood.

FATAL FACTS

The war was one of the deadliest in history. No one knows exactly how many people died. Historians estimate that at least 8 million soldiers died. Millions of civilians died as well.

■ **Many soldiers were buried in cemeteries near the battlefields.**

A MODERN WAR

World War I was different from previous wars. In many ways, it was the first modern war. New weapons, such as tanks and poison gas, killed many soldiers. Planes took off from aircraft carriers to launch bombing raids. Wireless radios allowed armies to communicate better. Army doctors were able to use X-rays to help treat the wounded.

Why Did the War Start?

It took one Serbian teenager just two shots to set off World War I. On June 28, 1914, Gavrilo Princip killed Franz Ferdinand, the heir to the throne of Austria-Hungary. Within a month, Austria-Hungary and Serbia were at war. Another month later, a dozen countries were involved, and fighting had begun.

■ Princip was arrested after the assassination. He later died in prison.

FATAL FACTS

Gavrilo Princip was linked to a secret group called the Black Hand. They wanted to unify all lands where Serbs lived into a single kingdom. This would mean taking lands that belonged to other countries. The Black Hand had already murdered people to get what they wanted.

Problems in Europe had been brewing for years. The **assassination** was the trigger needed to start a war. A rise in nationalism (the belief that you should put your country's interests above those of others) made countries aggressive. The United Kingdom and France had **colonies** in other parts of the world, such as Africa. Colonies' natural resources made them sources of power and wealth. Germany wanted a colonial empire too.

ARMS RACE

Since the turn of the century, Germany and the United Kingdom had been involved in an arms race. The United Kingdom's navy was the most powerful in the world. Germany wanted to build a fleet just as strong. They also increased the size of their army. Other countries were arming themselves too.

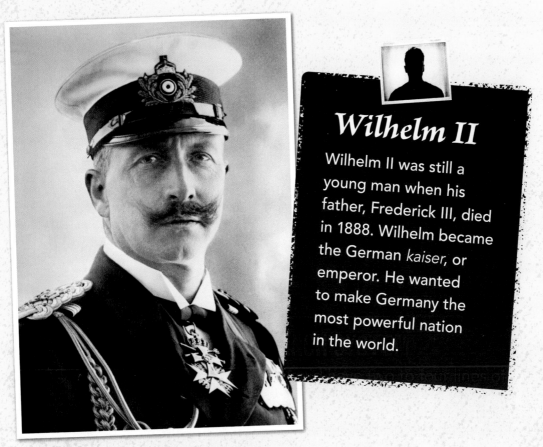

Wilhelm II

Wilhelm II was still a young man when his father, Frederick III, died in 1888. Wilhelm became the German *kaiser*, or emperor. He wanted to make Germany the most powerful nation in the world.

A TANGLED WEB

Europe's countries were linked by a complicated web of **treaties**. Germany, Austria-Hungary, and Italy formed the Triple Alliance in 1882. They agreed that if one were attacked, the others would come to its defense. Together, they would be a powerful opponent.

France, the United Kingdom, and Russia were worried. They formed their own alliance, called the Triple Entente. The biggest nations in Europe were now lined up on two sides. There were already rumblings of conflict. Russia, Italy, and Austria-Hungary wanted more influence in the Balkans.

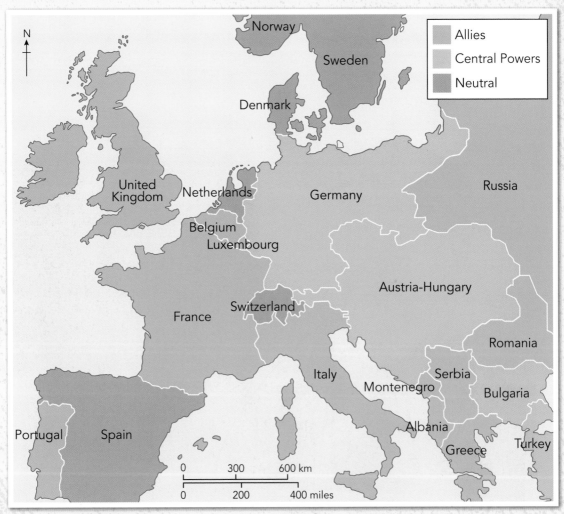

■ Some European countries stayed neutral. The others were divided into the Allies and the Central Powers.

THE WAR BEGINS

After Franz Ferdinand's murder, Austria-Hungary wanted to declare war on Serbia. But they knew that Russia supported Serbia. Combined with its **allies** (France and the United Kingdom), Russia would be tough to beat. But Germany promised to support Austria-Hungary. Both countries thought they could win. Then they would divide up the defeated lands.

Nicholas II

Nicholas II was the tsar of Russia. King George V of the United Kingdom and Wilhelm II of Germany were his first cousins. The three men had the same grandmother: Queen Victoria. Nicholas was assassinated in 1918, shortly after Russia pulled out of the war.

LINING UP

At the start, the two sides were fairly evenly balanced. Germany had the biggest, best-trained army. The United Kingdom had a small army, but it had a powerful navy. The Allied countries had easier access to the Atlantic Ocean. This meant they could get supplies from **neutral** countries, such as the United States.

LAND ARMY SIZES IN AUGUST 1914

Germany	Russia	France	Austria-Hungary	United Kingdom
1.9 million	**1.4 million**	**1.29 million**	**450,000**	**120,000**

BUILDING ARMIES

At first, huge numbers of men volunteered to serve. For example, in the United Kingdom, there were nearly 500,000 volunteers in the first six weeks of the war. France and the United Kingdom also got soldiers from their overseas colonies. Troops arrived from Canada, Australia, New Zealand, and parts of Africa.

LORD KITCHENER SAYS:-

'MEN, MATERIALS & MONEY ARE THE IMMEDIATE NECESSITIES. ......

DOES THE CALL OF DUTY FIND NO RESPONSE IN YOU UNTIL REINFORCED — LET US RATHER SAY SUPERSEDED — BY THE CALL OF COMPULSION ?'

Lord Kitchener Speaking at Guildhall July 9th 1915

ENLIST TO-DAY.

■ A photo of Herbert Kitchener, the U.K. War Minister in 1914, appeared on many posters encouraging young men to join the army.

Some countries used **conscription**. In Germany, men had to join the army at age 20 and train for two or three years. After they were finished, they could be called back if war came. In August 1914, the German army did just that. The army went from 808,000 to 3.5 million in just two weeks.

THE UNITED STATES ENTERS

When war broke out, the United States stayed neutral. Most Americans thought that the war was a European problem. They provided supplies to the Allies, but no troops. But then the Germans started sinking American ships. The U.S. entered the war in April 1917.

FATAL FACTS

Millions of animals were used by both sides. Trained pigeons carried messages. Horses, donkeys, oxen, and camels pulled heavy carts carrying supplies. Horses were an important resource, so soldiers took good care of them. Some even had their own gas masks! Even so, historians estimate that several million horses were killed.

What Weapons Did Soldiers Use?

The war was fought with weapons both large and small. Some of them, such as rifles, were not new. Many rifles had a short blade called a bayonet attached to the end of the barrel. The bayonet let the rifle be used both as a gun and as a sword.

There were new developments too. Trained German **snipers** had powerful rifles with **telescopic sights**. These helped them hit targets accurately from long range. They could pick off enemy soldiers who peered out of their **trenches**. The German snipers were very successful. The British army soon began training snipers too.

Learning to use a bayonet was part of a soldier's training.

HEAVY ARTILLERY

Foot soldiers were supported by their army's **artillery**. These huge guns had to be wheeled into place. They were usually hidden far behind the front lines. They fired heavy **shells** at enemy positions, several miles away. Hundreds of millions of shells were fired during the war.

The shells fired by artillery pieces killed more soldiers than any other weapon.

Some shells burst like dynamite, leaving huge craters. The sharp fragments of the shell flew through the air, causing injuries. Other shells were filled with tiny metal balls. When they exploded over enemy lines, the balls flew in all directions. They tore into soldiers' flesh.

MACHINE GUNS

The most common rifles could fire up to 30 shots per minute. They were no match for machine guns, which could fire 500. These guns were invented in the 1860s, but they came into their own during this war. A single machine gun could mow down rows of attacking soldiers.

These machine guns were too big and heavy for a soldier to carry. They were operated by a crew of 4–6 soldiers. Bullets were fed in along a fabric belt or metal strip. Early versions often jammed or overheated. Engineers designed cooling systems to keep them from overheating.

DEADLY FIRE

Machine gunners used something called "enfilade fire." They positioned their guns on the sides of the battlefield. This meant they fired almost sideways at the attacking troops. Trained gun crews could inflict huge losses this way.

MAXIM MACHINE GUN

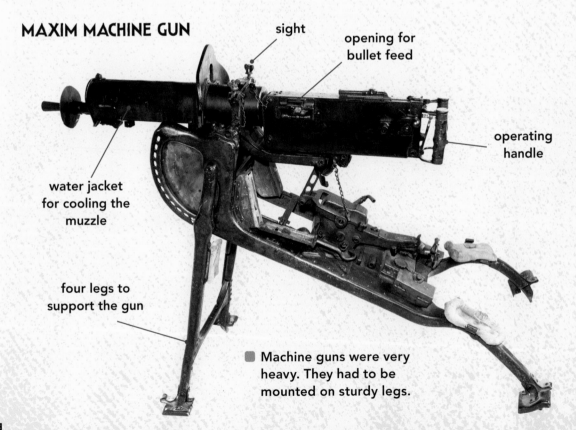

sight

opening for bullet feed

operating handle

water jacket for cooling the muzzle

four legs to support the gun

◼ Machine guns were very heavy. They had to be mounted on sturdy legs.

A single grenade tossed into an enemy trench could kill several soldiers when it exploded. The German army used one with a wooden handle. This meant it could be thrown farther. Australian soldiers made their own grenades by packing explosives into jam tins.

SHEETS OF FIRE

In July 1915, German soldiers used flamethrowers against British troops. These machines shot burning oil up to 60 feet (18 meters). Some were large, but smaller versions could be carried by a single man. They terrified soldiers when they were first used. The Germans sent flamethrowers ahead of attacking foot soldiers. They could clear the front ranks of the defenders.

Flamethrowers could inflict horrible burns.

This cartoon appeared in a French newspaper, condemning Germany's use of poison gas.

Fritz Haber

Fritz Haber was a German chemist. He led the team that developed chlorine gas and other chemical weapons. He also helped design gas masks to protect soldiers. He witnessed the German army's use of chlorine gas in April 1915.

DEADLY GAS

In October 1914, some artillery guns began to fire shells filled with gas. It was tear gas, which was fairly harmless. The following spring, the German army used chlorine gas against French troops. It made the soldiers cough and choke when they breathed it in.

Both sides used gas during the war. If the wind changed, it could blow back on their own troops. This happened to British troops at Loos, France, in September 1915. Some types of gas attacked soldiers' lungs and airways. Mustard gas caused vomiting, skin blisters, and bleeding. Overall, about 90,000 soldiers were killed by gas during the war. Many others took years to recover after being caught in gas attacks.

HISTORY UNLOCKED

When gas was first used, soldiers had no way to protect themselves. They soon started wearing gas masks. The masks used charcoal and chemicals to filter out the harmful gas. However, they were uncomfortable to wear, and often fogged up.

THE BIRTH OF THE TANK

World War I was the first time that tanks were used in battle. These tough vehicles had heavy armor for protection. Their caterpillar tracks took them across rough ground or over trenches. Nearly 500 tanks were used in one battle in 1917, proving their usefulness.

What Was Life Like in the Trenches?

In the first months, the war moved quickly. Germany attacked aggressively, invading Luxembourg and Belgium before moving into France. The two sides then started racing north, toward the sea. Each wanted to get around the enemy's lines, but neither was able to. Within just a few months, the two sides were dug into a long line of trenches.

In trench warfare, both sides made use of semi-permanent trenches dug into the ground. They were necessary because of the power of artillery and machine guns. The troops needed a place to take shelter.

■ Conditions were cramped and dirty in trenches, and an attack could come at any time.

THE TRENCH SYSTEM

An army would have two to four lines of trenches running parallel to each other. They were deep enough for men to stand up, and they were protected by barbed wire and sandbags. The front trench was the first line of defence. Many of these trenches had a zigzag pattern. If enemy soldiers got in, they could not fire far along the trench.

Shorter trenches connected the front trench to the ones at the rear. Supplies and fresh soldiers would get to the front this way. The whole system was sometimes several miles deep. Behind the trenches, the heavy artillery lined up. On the other side, the enemy's trench system stretched out like a mirror image. Between the two lines was an empty expanse called **"no-man's-land."**

■ This model shows how trenches were connected to each other.

FATAL FACTS

Rats were a huge problem in trenches. They would eat food supplies as well as dead bodies, growing fat and bold. They would sometimes run across soldiers' faces while they slept.

WHERE A TRENCH SOLDIER SPENT HIS TIME

Behind the lines	Rear reserve trench	Middle support trench	Front-line trench
45%	**30%**	**10%**	**15%**

ATTACKING A TRENCH

Trenches were not easy to capture. Before a large attack, an army would use their artillery. They would shell the enemy positions for hours, or even days. The goal was to destroy the defenses to clear the way for the **infantry** (foot soldiers). The infantry then had to leave the relative safety of their own trench. They would face heavy fire from the enemy trench.

Wave after wave of soldiers would cross no-man's-land. They had to avoid machine gun fire and get through the barbed wire protecting the enemy trenches. If they gained ground, they had to dig new trenches to defend it. These large-scale attacks were rarely very successful.

Going "over the top" exposed a soldier to enemy fire. It must have been terrifying.

SNEAKING IN

Armies soon tried other ways of attacking trenches. They would send small groups to slip through weak points in the enemy line. They would break up the line, leaving it more open to infantry attack. Another tactic was to dig tunnels across no-man's-land. Once the tunnel reached beneath the enemy trenches, explosives would destroy them.

FATAL FACTS

The land of Belgium and northern France is flat and wet. Mud was a huge problem for soldiers on both sides. Horses, wheeled vehicles, and shells churned up the mud. Countless soldiers and horses drowned in it.

HISTORY UNLOCKED

At Christmas 1914, everyone serving in the British forces received one of these boxes. The boxes contained gifts such as cigarettes, chocolates, pencils, a comb, postcards, scissors — and a Christmas card. They were paid for by public donations.

MAJOR BATTLES

On the Western Front, battles could last for months, claiming hundreds of thousands of lives. The Battle of Verdun lasted for most of 1916. The Germans wanted to gain ground, but they also wanted to kill enough French soldiers to destroy their **morale**. In the end, the French were able to block the attack. About 300,000 soldiers were killed, with another 450,000 wounded.

The Battle of the Somme began late in 1916. The Allied artillery pounded the German lines for a week before the infantry attacked. But the German defenses had not been seriously damaged. They killed huge numbers of the attacking troops.

HISTORY UNLOCKED

Here is how a French soldier remembered the Battle of Verdun:

"Day after day pounded by artillery, peering with bleary eyes through the dust and smoke, the earth rocking drunkenly, trenches flattened out and smashed. And then the Boche [Germans] attack."

The Battle of Verdun utterly destroyed the local area.

DROWNING IN MUD

In 1917, the Battle of Passchendaele left about 500,000 soldiers dead or injured. The area had already been the scene of much fighting. Shell craters pockmarked the land. More shelling, mixed with heavy rain, turned it into a dangerous sea of mud.

■ At Passchendaele, stretcher-bearers struggled through the mud to get the wounded to safety.

THE BATTLE OF THE SOMME BY THE NUMBERS

The Battle of the Somme took place along a
15 mile line.

At the start, more than
100,000
Allied soldiers attacked the German lines.

On the first day,
19,240
British soldiers died. More than
38,000 were wounded.

By the end, over
1,000,000
soldiers (from both sides) had been killed or wounded.

The battle lasted
141 days.

The Allied armies had advanced only
7 miles.

What Happened at Sea and in the Air?

The main battles of the war took place on land. However, there were also some fought at sea. In the years before the war, Germany had built up its navy. It wanted to be as powerful as the British Royal Navy. Both sides built bigger and better ships. New technology made them faster, and they had powerful guns.

BLOCKADE

These giant warships only met in one large battle. Instead of battles, both sides' navies concentrated on **blockades**. The Allies wanted to block trade ships from reaching Germany. A lack of food and raw materials would weaken their enemy. British ships patrolled the North Sea to make sure no one got through.

FATAL FACTS

German U-boats (submarines) targeted ships bringing supplies to the Allied nations. U-boats could approach unseen before launching torpedoes. Over the course of the war, U-boats sank about 5,000 ships.

Being a submariner was dangerous. About 5,000 German sailors were killed when their U-boats went down.

THE BATTLE OF JUTLAND

The biggest battle between the British and German fleets took place on May 31, 1916. They met off the coast of Denmark. After a day of heavy fighting, 25 ships had been sunk. Neither side really won the battle. Germany sank more enemy ships, but the Royal Navy kept control of the North Sea.

■ When a large warship sank, most of its crew was often killed.

John Jellicoe

Admiral John Jellicoe was in charge of the British fleet. After the Battle of Jutland, many people criticized him. They thought that the Royal Navy should have been able to win a crushing victory.

THE BATTLE OF JUTLAND BY THE NUMBERS

Britain
151 ships
14 sunk

6,094 killed
851 wounded

Germany
99 ships
11 sunk

2,551 killed
507 wounded

FIGHTING IN THE AIR

The Wright brothers made the first airplane flight in 1903. Just over a decade later, the war began. At first, many generals were skeptical about this new technology. They mainly used planes for observation missions. Airplanes could fly over enemy lines to learn about their defenses. They took photos, which helped the artillery find their targets.

These early planes were made of wood covered in fabric. Their pilots carried pistols, but the planes themselves were often not armed. Then in 1915, the Germans perfected a new device. It allowed a machine gun to fire through the propeller without smashing the blades. This gave them a huge advantage — until the other side developed their own.

ZEPPELINS

Huge airships called **zeppelins** were used for passenger travel before the war. Now they were pressed into service. Some were used for spying and some as bombers. Zeppelins dropped bombs on cities in the United Kingdom and France. They also bombed important ports and factories.

■ Zeppelins were slow and made easy targets for fighter planes.

A DANGEROUS JOB

Life as a pilot in the war was very dangerous. Planes could be unreliable, and many pilots were killed in training crashes. They faced attack from enemy aircraft and from defenders firing from the ground. Once the German pilots were able to fire machine guns, life expectancy for an Allied pilot dropped to 17.5 hours of flying time.

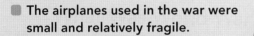 The airplanes used in the war were small and relatively fragile.

The Red Baron

Many wartime pilots became celebrities. The most famous was Germany's Manfred von Richthofen. He was known as the "Red Baron" because of his red airplane. He shot down 80 enemy aircraft before being shot down and killed in 1918.

How Many Fronts Were There?

When most people think of World War I, they think of the trenches on the Western Front. However, the war was much bigger than that. There was fierce fighting in Eastern Europe, Africa, Asia, and the Middle East.

THE EASTERN FRONT

The armies of the Central Powers were fighting on two sides. To the west, they faced the armies of France and the United Kingdom. To the east, they fought the powerful Russian army. This "Eastern Front" was much bigger than the Western Front. It also moved more than the Western Front. Large areas of Eastern Europe were scarred by fighting.

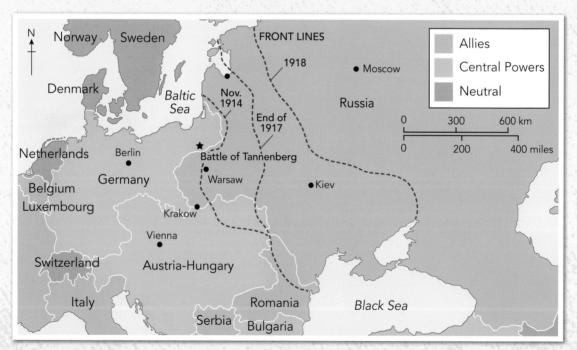

■ The Eastern Front stretched from the Baltic Sea in the north all the way to the Black Sea.

SUPPLY PROBLEMS

The Eastern Front covered such a large area that keeping troops supplied was a big problem. Armies relied on trains to bring supplies. If they advanced too far from their railroads, they couldn't get fresh troops, food, and **ammunition**.

FATAL FACTS

Casualties were high on the Eastern Front. At Tannenberg in 1914, Russia suffered a crushing defeat against Germany. About 30,000 of their soldiers were killed or wounded. Another 90,000 or more were taken prisoner. The Germans captured so much military equipment that they needed 60 trains to take it all back to Germany.

RUSSIA PULLS OUT

Even before the war started, Russia had political and economic problems. These got worse once the fighting began. Resources were sent to the army instead of feeding the people. A revolution in 1917 overthrew the tsar. Russia's new leaders soon signed a treaty with Germany.

■ Soldiers on the Eastern Front had to deal with mountainous terrain and deep snow.

WAR IN THE MIDDLE EAST

The Ottoman Empire, based in Turkey, had ruled large parts of the Middle East for centuries. In 1914, it entered the war alongside the Central Powers. Ottoman ships attacked Russian ports in the Black Sea. Russia, France, and the United Kingdom declared war on the Ottoman Empire.

The Middle East and Africa were important regions for the European powers. African colonies were rich in natural resources. Oilfields in Iraq and elsewhere provided much-needed fuel. The Suez Canal — controlled by Britain — was a crucial trade route. In 1915, Ottoman troops tried to seize the canal but failed.

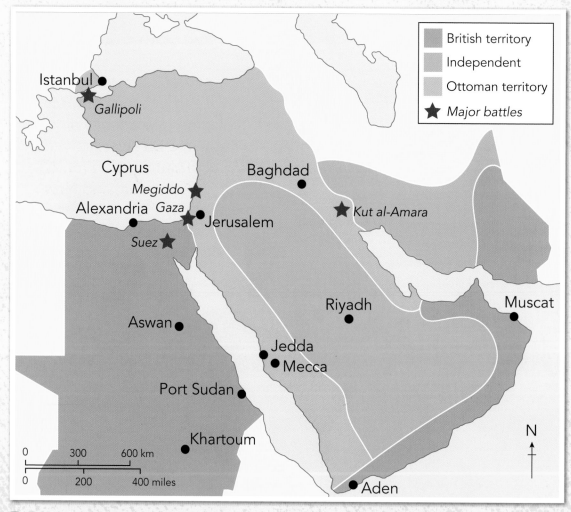

British territory
Independent
Ottoman territory
★ Major battles

Istanbul
Gallipoli
Cyprus
Baghdad
Megiddo
Alexandria Gaza
Jerusalem
Kut al-Amara
Suez
Riyadh
Muscat
Aswan
Jedda
Mecca
Port Sudan
Khartoum
N
0   300   600 km
0   200   400 miles
Aden

■ This map shows some of the main battles in Africa and the Middle East.

GALLIPOLI

A narrow strait called the Dardanelles separates the Black Sea and the Mediterranean Sea. The Ottomans had control of it. Russian navy ships in the Black Sea couldn't get out, and Allied ships bringing supplies to Russia couldn't get in.

THE DAILY MIRROR, Thursday, July 15, 1915.

ALLIES CAPTURE IMPORTANT POSITIONS IN DARD...

The Daily Mirror

CERTIFIED CIRCULATION LARGER THAN ANY OTHER PICTURE PAPER IN THE WORLD

No. 3,658. Registered at the G.P.O. as a Newspaper. THURSDAY, JULY 15, 1915. One Halfpenny.

BRITISH OFFICER LEADS AN ATTACK: A CHARGE BY THE NAVAL DIVISION ON THE GALLIPOLI PENINSULA.

Among the units which are adding such glorious pages to our history in the Dardanelles is the Royal Naval Division, and in this photograph they are seen leaping from their trench to charge the Turks. An officer is leading the men. The photograph also gives an idea of the nature of the country. Nature would seem to have designed it with a | view to the defence of Constantinople, but this only adds lustre to the glorious feats of arms which have been accomplished against a brave enemy. The news from the peninsula continues good, and the report of another important success reached London yesterday. Other Dardanelles pictures appear on pages 6 and 7.

The Royal Navy attacked, but failed to take control of the Dardanelles. Then British, French, Australian, and New Zealand troops landed on the Gallipoli peninsula to take out the enemy defenses. For months, they were pinned down on the beaches before finally pulling out. Each side had suffered about 250,000 casualties.

■ Newspapers kept people at home up to date with Gallipoli and other battles.

How Did the War Affect Civilians?

The war had a huge impact on civilian life. Even outside the fighting zone, daily life changed. Ordinary civilians — such as Germans living in the United States — could be seen as "enemy aliens." Some of these people had their movement restricted. Others were sent to **internment camps** for the rest of the war.

REPLACING SOLDIERS

In many places, so many men were off fighting that the workforce was too small. Women stepped up to fill many of these roles. Women served as police officers, bus drivers, postal workers, and farmers. Many worked in munitions factories, producing weapons and ammunition. Others joined the military as nurses, cooks, or mechanics.

■ Women in munitions factories did jobs that had previously been done by men.

KEEPING CALM

Life could be hard on the home front. Civilians worried about loved ones fighting overseas. They sometimes even came under attack themselves. Zeppelin bombing raids killed about 1,500 British civilians during the war. Although that number is small, the raids spread fear and panic.

Lusitania Sinking, the Greatest of Ocean Tragedies

THE LUSITANIA, WHICH SAILED FROM NEW YORK FOR LIVERPOOL MAY 1, 1915, WITH 1,959 SOULS ON BOARD, WAS SUNK BY A GERMAN SUBMARINE MAY 7, WITH A LOSS, INCLUDING WOMEN AND CHILDREN, OF 1,195.

HISTORY UNLOCKED

The *Lusitania* was a British passenger ship. In May 1915, it was sailing from New York to Liverpool. It was torpedoed by a German U-boat and sank, killing almost 1,200 people. This newspaper report shows how horrified many Americans were at what they saw as German ruthlessness.

WAITING FOR NEWS

Many newspapers tried to keep morale up by glossing over bad news. For example, British newspapers didn't print pictures of dead British soldiers. However, many newspapers printed lists of those killed or wounded. Families at home would read these, hoping not to see a loved one's name.

LIFE IN A WAR ZONE

Life was hard for people who lived near the fronts. Millions of people were forced from their homes, or saw their farms and businesses destroyed. When a foreign army invaded, many civilians fled and became refugees. Others were forced out or taken prisoner.

FORCED LABOR

In occupied regions, the invaders controlled civilian life. People in these areas were sometimes used as forced labor. Both sides were guilty of forcing civilians and prisoners to work. They worked on farms or building roads. Many worked in factories.

■ Hundreds of thousands of refugees ended up living in makeshift camps.

SHORTAGES

The war used huge amounts of resources. Soldiers at the front needed food, uniforms, weapons, and fuel. This often meant that people back home had to go without. It was an especially big problem for Germany. The Allied naval blockade kept supplies from abroad from arriving. Food shortages were very common across Europe. Many farms had been destroyed. Others were short of workers and fertilizer. In some places, food shortages led to riots as people starved.

FATAL FACTS

The land that is now Armenia was part of the Ottoman Empire. The Muslim Ottomans didn't trust Armenians, who were mainly Christian. They thought they might side with their enemies. During and after the war, the Ottomans carried out **genocide** against the Armenians. About 1.5 million people died.

HISTORY UNLOCKED

Several countries started **rationing** food, to make sure that it was shared fairly. In Germany, bread was rationed first. Civilians were given books of coupons that allowed them to buy only a certain amount of bread. Potatoes, butter, sugar, meat, eggs, and milk were also rationed.

What Role Did Medicine Play?

Weapons like machine guns weren't the only killers during the war. Illnesses caused huge numbers of deaths. In fact, some countries saw more soldiers die of disease than be killed in action. Army doctors had to do their best to keep soldiers healthy. A soldier needing treatment would be carried on a stretcher to the rear lines. Doctors would decide whether to treat him there or send him to hospital.

■ Hospital trains took injured or ill soldiers back to a base hospital for care.

COMMON DISEASES

Many men were packed close together in muddy, dirty trenches. These conditions were perfect for spreading disease. Illnesses such as typhus, **influenza**, and dysentery were common. At the time, there were few medicines available to treat these diseases.

Trench fever was spread by the body lice that infested the trenches. It gave soldiers a high fever, aching muscles, and sores on the skin. It could take 2–3 months to recover. Many soldiers caught trench fever more than once. Trench life could also cause a condition called trench foot. Standing in cold water or mud for long periods made feet swell, or go numb and painful. Some soldiers had to have their feet **amputated** as a result.

FATAL FACTS

In the spring of 1918, the end of the war was in sight. Then a deadly strain of influenza swept the world. It infected about one-third of the world's people. The "Spanish flu" raged until summer of 1919. It may have killed 50 million people, and possibly more.

■ Soldiers were told to gargle with saltwater to prevent influenza.

DEATH TOLLS THROUGH WAR AND FLU

Soldiers in WWI: 65 million took part, of which 8 million were killed

Influenza epidemic: 500 million infected, of which 50 million were killed

INJURIES AND INFECTION

On the front lines, shell fragments and bullets tore into soldiers' bodies. The mud and filth of the battlefield meant that these wounds often got infected. Antibiotics had not been discovered yet, so people could die from fairly minor injuries. Because of this, amputations were common. Hundreds of thousands of soldiers lost arms or legs.

■ Doctors on the front lines had to work in difficult conditions.

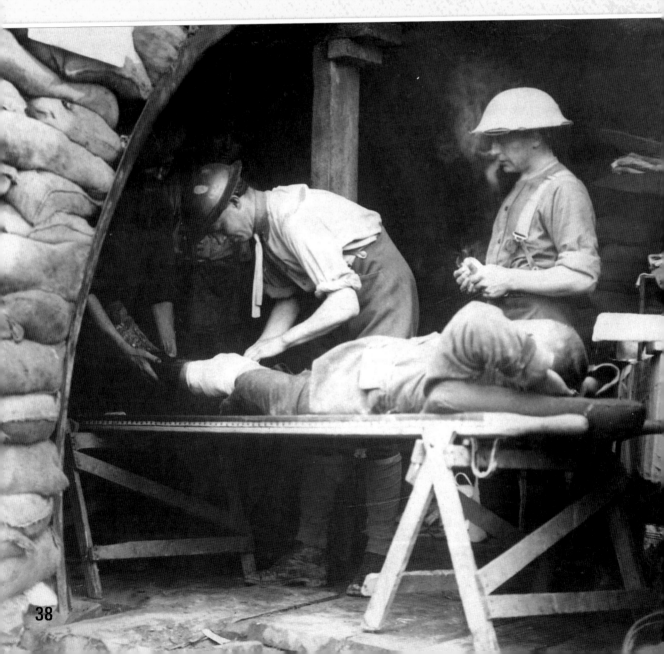

SHELL SHOCK

A soldier's life during wartime was dangerous and upsetting. They had to deal with fear, losing friends, and taking human lives. Many soldiers broke down under the strain. This condition was known as "**shell shock**." Soldiers with shell shock might be unable to speak or eat. They might have nightmares or facial tics. Some senior officers had little sympathy. They thought that these men were showing weakness in the face of danger.

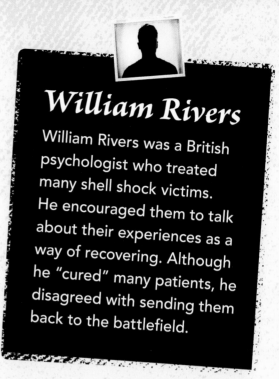

William Rivers

William Rivers was a British psychologist who treated many shell shock victims. He encouraged them to talk about their experiences as a way of recovering. Although he "cured" many patients, he disagreed with sending them back to the battlefield.

BACK TO THE FRONT LINES

Army doctors tried to get wounded soldiers back to the trenches as quickly as possible. But many soldiers were too seriously wounded to fight again. They would be sent home and receive a **pension**. They were often too badly injured to go back to their old jobs.

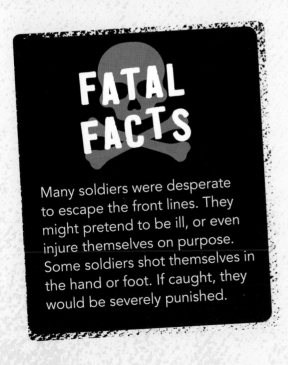

FATAL FACTS

Many soldiers were desperate to escape the front lines. They might pretend to be ill, or even injure themselves on purpose. Some soldiers shot themselves in the hand or foot. If caught, they would be severely punished.

Many soldiers who lost legs were never able to go back to work.

How Did the War End?

In March 1918, Russia signed a treaty with the Central Powers and left the war. German soldiers on the Eastern Front were now free to fight in the west. However, more Allied soldiers were arriving every day. They included many from the United States. If the Germans wanted victory, they needed to act fast.

The Germans launched a huge surprise attack. They outnumbered the Allies, and they advanced quickly. But by July, they were running short of troops and supplies. Both sides had lost hundreds of thousands of soldiers. The Allied forces had more troops to replace them; the Germans did not.

■ When American soldiers arrived, their numbers helped turn the tide.

FATAL FACTS

Between August and November 1918, the Allies threw everything they had at the Germans. They suffered huge losses. About one-third of the British troops then serving on the Western Front were killed or wounded.

TURNING THE TIDE

In August, the Allies launched their own attack. Slowly but surely, they pushed the Germans back. At the same time, Germany was in chaos. Ordinary people wanted the war to end, and the Kaiser had to step down. On November 11, 1918, German and Allied leaders signed an **armistice**. The war was over.

■ Douglas Haig was a British general. In his diary for November 11, he noted that it was a "fine day, but cold and dull."

What Were the Effects of the War?

The Allies and the Germans signed the Treaty of Versailles in 1919. It treated Germany harshly. They had to give up some of their territory. They also had to reduce their army and pay compensation. The map of Europe now looked very different. Borders were redrawn, and new countries — such as Poland and Czechoslovakia — appeared.

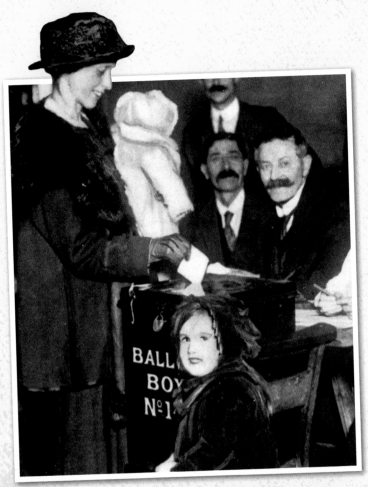

A NEW WORLD

There were changes on the home front as well. Working women had made a real difference during the war. Some kept working, but many had to give up their jobs when the soldiers came home. Women in the United Kingdom, U.S., Russia, and Germany were finally given the right to vote shortly after the war.

■ Women over 30 voted for the first time in the United Kingdom in 1918.

A WAR TO END ALL WARS?

The war had been incredibly destructive. Millions of people were dead, and homes and factories had been destroyed. No one wanted another world war. Several countries set up a group called the League of Nations. Its goal was to resolve international conflict peacefully.

However, the United States never joined, and Germany and Russia left in the 1930s. Many Germans were angry about their country's harsh treatment. The League's power was limited, and it was not able to stop the world from heading toward another world war, just 20 years later.

■ **War memorials in many countries record the names of the dead.**

HISTORY UNLOCKED

President Woodrow Wilson gave this speech in support of the League of Nations.

"Unless you get the united, concerted purpose and power of the great governments of the world behind this settlement, it will fall down like a house of cards. There is only one power to put behind the liberation of mankind, and that is the power of mankind."

Timeline

1914

June 28	Gavrilo Princip kills Archduke Franz Ferdinand.
July 28	Austria-Hungary declares war on Serbia.
August 1	Germany declares war on Russia.
August 3	Germany declares war on France.
August 4	Germany invades Belgium. The United Kingdom declares war on Germany.
August 17	The first battle on the Eastern Front takes place.
August 23–30	The Battle of Tannenberg ends in heavy Russian losses.
October 22	The race to the sea ends. The Western Front lines are now set.
October 29	The Ottoman Empire attacks Russia.
November 3	The Allied naval blockade of Germany begins.

1915

January 19	The Germans launch the first zeppelin raid on the United Kingdom.
February 19	British and French troops attack the Ottomans at Gallipoli.
April 22–May 25	The Germans first use poison gas at the Second Battle of Ypres.
May 7	The passenger ship *Lusitania* is sunk by a German U-boat.
September 25–28	The British launch a failed offensive at Loos.

1916

January 9	The Gallipoli campaign ends in failure for the Allied troops.
February 21	The Battle of Verdun begins.
May 31–June 1	The largest naval battle of the war takes place at Jutland.
July 1	The Battle of the Somme begins.
September 15–22	At the Battle of Flers-Courcelette, the British use tanks for the first time.
November 18	The battle of the Somme ends; French and British troops have gained ground.
December 18	The Battle of Verdun finally ends with huge losses on both sides.

1917

March 15	Nicholas II of Russia gives up his throne.
April 6	The United States declares war on Germany.
June 25	The first American troops arrive in France.
July 31–November 10	The Battle of Passchendaele takes place.

1918

March 3	The new Russian government signs a peace treaty with Germany.
March 21	Germany launches the Spring Offensive on the Western Front.
July 17	Nicholas II and his family are killed.
August 8	The Allied Hundred Days Offensive begins.
November 9	Kaiser Wilhelm II steps down as ruler of Germany.
November 11	Armistice between Germany and the Allies is signed.

GLOSSARY

ally (AL-eye)—a person or country that helps and supports another

ammunition (am-yuh-NI-shuhn)—bullets and other objects that can be fired from weapons

amputate (AM-pyuh-tayt)—to cut off someone's arm, leg, or other body part

armistice (AR-miss-tiss)—formal agreement to end the fighting of a war

artillery (ar-TI-luhr-ee)—cannons and other large guns used during battles

assassination (uh-sass-uh-NAY-shun)—the murder of someone who is well known or important

blockade (blok-AYD)—a closing off of an area to keep people or supplies from going in or out

casualty (KAZH-oo-uhl-tee)—someone who is injured, captured, killed, or missing in a war

chlorine gas (KLOR-een)—poisonous gas that attacks a person's lungs and airway

civilian (si-VIL-yuhn)—a person who is not in the military

colony (KAH-luh-nee)—a place that is settled by people from another country and is controlled by that country

conscription (kuhn-SKRIP-shun)—a forced military draft

genocide (JEN-oh-side)—to destroy a race of people on purpose

infantry (IN-fuhn-tree)—a group of soldiers trained to fight and travel on foot

influenza (in-floo-EN-zuh)—an illness that is like a bad cold with fever and muscle pain; a virus causes influenza.

internment camp (in-TERN-ment KAMP)—place where civilians are kept (by force) because they are seen to be a danger during war

morale (muh-RAL)—a person or group's feelings or state of mind

neutral (NOO-truhl)—not taking any side in a war

no-man's-land (NOH-MANZ-LAND)—the area between enemy trenches where most of the fighting (and dying) took place

pension (PEN-shuhn)—money paid regularly to a retired person

primary source (PRYE-mair-ee SORSS)—source from someone who experienced an event firsthand

ration (RASH-uhn)—to limit to prevent running out of something

shell (SHEL)—a hollow cartridge filled with an explosive that will explode on contact with a target

shell shock (SHEL SHOK)—mental disturbance caused by exposure to the horrors of war

sniper (SNY-pur)—a soldier trained to shoot at long-distance targets from a hidden place

telescopic sight (TEL-uh-SKOP-ik SITE)—small telescope mounted on a rifle that helps the shooter aim

treaty (TREE-tee)—an official agreement between two or more groups or countries

trench (TRENCH)—a long, narrow ditch dug in the ground to serve as shelter from enemy fire or attack

zeppelin (ZEP-lin)—a large oval-shaped airship with a rigid frame; zeppelins are named for their inventor, Count Ferdinand von Zeppelin.

READ MORE

Books

Hunter, Nick. *Campaigns of World War I.* Remembering World War I. Chicago: Heinemann-Raintree, 2014.

Micklos, John. *Harlem Hellfighters: African-American Heroes of World War I.* Military Heroes. Mankato, Minn.: Capstone Press, 2017.

Powley, Adam. *World War I Close Up.* The War Chronicles. New York: Rosen Publishing, 2016.

Rissman, Rebecca. *World War I: Why They Fought.* What Were They Fighting For? Mankato, Minn.: Compass Point Books, 2016.

Steele, Philip. *Did Anything Good Come Out of World War I?* Innovation Through Adversity. New York: Rosen Publishing, 2016.

Internet Sites

FactHound offers a safe, fun way to find Internet sites related to this book. All of the sites on FactHound have been researched by our staff.

Here's all you do:

Visit *www.facthound.com*

Type in this code: 9781484641682

Places to Visit

National Museum of American History
Constitution Avenue, NW
Washington, D.C. 20001
http://americanhistory.si.edu

National WWI Museum and Memorial
2 Memorial Drive
Kansas City, MO 64108
https://www.theworldwar.org

Vintage Aero Flying Museum
7125 Parks Lane
Fort Lupton, CO 80621
http://www.vafm.org

Critical Thinking Questions

Which parts of this book did you find the most interesting? What subjects would you like to know more about?

How did the network of treaties between European countries help contribute to the scale of the war?

Describe how conditions for soldiers on the Western Front differed from conditions for soldiers on the Eastern Front, or from sailors in the navies. Support your answer using information from at least two other texts or valid Internet sources.

Why was the United States so reluctant to enter the war? What helped to turn the tide of public opinion? Support your answer using information from at least two other texts or valid Internet sources.

INDEX